I0829808

# African Jungle Women Living Life

## Just Living

Ian C. Kenson

authorHOUSE®

*AuthorHouse™ UK*
*1663 Liberty Drive*
*Bloomington, IN 47403  USA*
*www.authorhouse.co.uk*
*Phone: 0800.197.4150*



*Published by AuthorHouse 02/13/2019*

*ISBN: 978-1-7283-8465-8 (sc)*
*ISBN: 978-1-7283-8464-1 (e)*

*Print information available on the last page.*

*Any people depicted in stock imagery provided by Getty Images are models, and such images are being used for illustrative purposes only. Certain stock imagery © Getty Images.*

*This book is printed on acid-free paper.*

*Because of the dynamic nature of the Internet, any web addresses or links contained in this book may have changed since publication and may no longer be valid. The views expressed in this work are solely those of the author and do not necessarily reflect the views of the publisher, and the publisher hereby disclaims any responsibility for them.*

# CONTENTS

# Introduction

When I initially thought of penning this dramatically sad living experience, I seriously considered who would be remotely interested in it. Obviously, it could be verbally stated and suggested to naturally considerate and caring people, along with others who would require specific knowledge because of the employment and the location through their companies needs and demands, whilst ignoring the simple plight of every remotely living families, should if ever they had a choice or say who would be allowed to plunder their eons old spits of land, that profits the rulers of their country, thereby giving no choice.

These vast and specific areas, throughout the tropical areas of the world, are by nature the exact opposite of the extreme desert areas of the world. They have unlimited water in which mangroves grow in abundance, thrusting their roots deep into the swampland ground, leaving little to no land on which people and populations can establish clearances that they could utilize as living ground, all of which profits the elite and foreign investors, but never the living local population, who only live there because there are no other options.

Because of these specific locations, where old- and new-growth mangroves re-establish themselves every year, families and people have populated certain areas of slightly raised land, usually two to three feet above the high water levels at high tide. The jungle swamp population living from birth to death, they seldom if ever venture beyond the swamp limits, by the simple rule of lack of work and affordability.

By choice or by birth and needs, they live and function through whatever the elements and nature throw at them, stoically obeying the rules that swamps and jungles afford them. Their normality is that after darkness, it gets light, whilst after daylight, it gets dark. Unless they live within the populated area, they have no power source except naked oil lamps, and also maybe battery torches. These have to be renewed as the battery life fades. Consequently, all life is put on hold until daylight returns.

Whilst the rest of the people in the world live their lives by their areas and their location, these peoples exist on meagre strips of uninhabitable jungle land, always subject to every element and condition that these locations have throughout their simple, meagre lives.

# ONE

## HOME

Mosquitoes had been relentless throughout the night, flitting around from body to body following the human sweat scent. Humidity had been very high. Scratch marks were etched into exposed skin. Through the first light, it was clear that the old man's condition had not gotten better. While staring into the increasing light, the surrounding jungle swamp began to emerge.

Life had changed since the fair-skinned men had arrived. Every day, large and small boats would speed up and down the creeks, washing swamp water over the dry stretches of higher ground, making the terrain wet with mud, living with these conditions only brought further misery to the meagre high land dwellers, because there was no method of stopping the small wave from cascading through the tangled roots of the mangrove swamp trees, washing any and all small encrustations over the raised land.

As the higher spit of land was barely thirty-five metres by seventy-five metres, it left little to no room for building with anything other than what the swamp and jungle provided. Homes had always been made of the always-abundant branches or heavy sticks, pushed into the semi-dried muddy ground and covered with broad leaves, usually banana leaves.

# TWO

## THE BEGINNING

For more than thirty-five years, Sara Umbali had kept the home going, badgering him when branches or wood had decayed or rotted, replacing fractured leaves when the rain came in everywhere. This had been her life for all of those years, time and dimness had blotted most of her life from her memory, but sometimes as she shuffled around their home a flash of distant past would spring to mind, these lately had been of when she had been a young child, chasing through dense jungle clearings, screaming at the other young kids that had followed her, these memories often made her very sad, her family had made a living by foraging through the jungle, she had learned quickly which of the jungle trees and bushes would be good to collect fruit and berries from, life had been hard but liveable.

As she reached her ninth year, every thing had changer, her father had called her back into the village where the chief was arguing with her father, out of the corner of her eye she could see a small canoe tied at the swamp waters edge, a young strong looking man stood along side of the canoe, father and the chief continued to argue, hands were waved fists were shaken then silence, which would erupt again after a short period of quiet, after nearly the whole day an agreement had been met and some money had changed hands, finally they called the young girl across to the chief hut, the village chief just pointed at the young man who walked over taking her by the hand, placed her in the canoe and paddled away. Her life with him began, what happened next became her way of life.

At first he constantly pestered her seeking to attempt having sex with him, although he knew she was crossly under age, time and time again she steadfastly refused his advances, which became more intense as she began to age, attempting to render her acceptable through alcohol, which was always brewed by the village chief, through out time she managed to avoid all contact with the usual routine of nightly drinking, by boiling water and drinking that instead, this would slowly lead to him seeking comfort with the more agreeable women within the small community.

Never in all that time had she ever spoken to him directly. She just indicated and pointed.

He would always paddled off to collect what she wanted, returning with what he had caught or collected. Sometimes, he returned with a medium-sized fish, sometimes a medium-sized snake, and sometimes a small crocodile. It was always something that would make up a meal. And he always returned with the sticks and wood to repair their shelter.

This did not make her life easy, as every day, when it was light enough in the swamp; she had to prepare something for them to eat. This mainly depended on how many small fish he had caught.

She managed to keep the small fire burning. She would fan the embers and slowly add wood shavings until the flames caught the larger twigs. Then, she would hoist the cooking tin onto the bent stick over the fire and heat the swamp water laced with flaked fish. She would throw in some tree root bark she had found in the swamp, which gave the cooked fish a tangy flavour.

She often sat staring at the swamp water flowing past the muddy spit of land. Many times, she heard machines above her head, noisy with engine sounds. More often than not, the dimness of the jungle swamp would lighten, making the swamp trees easier to see.

The water often floated large hyacinths into the swamp's tangled mangrove roots, only to wash them out again when the swamp drained. The only difference was spotting the snakes and baby crocodiles before they reached the spit of land. This usually happened when food was available.

# THREE

## EXISTENCE LIVING

Day after day had become year after year she had been caring for the man who lived with her. Many suns and moons ago, she lived in a woodland village on the other side of the swamp, playing and running through the trees, until she was taken. She was taken away in a small canoe. They, Sara and the strong young man had paddled through creeks and streams and across rivers until they reached the muddy spit of land. She had lived here since that time. How long was that? She did not know. Sunrise and sunset were her only ways of measuring time.

Throughout the decades, not many local things had changed. The sticky heat of the jungle swamp and the mosquitoes and insects that bit and left sores had eventually become unnoticed by her. The season of the yearly time cycle was all that changed.

The rainy season was always the worst. Thunderstorms and heavy rains lasted eighty-seven days, never leaving time for things to dry out. The daily heat increased as the sun moved across the equator, first northward, then southward.

This year's storms had been more violent than any previously remembered. Highly destructive winds had raced through the swamp, leaving huge trees across the waterways. Movement became restrictive for those who tried to navigate through the shredded branches. The cyclone winds had ripped bark from the trunks of the jungle vegetation, blocking canoe and boat movement through the swamps. This stopped fishing, making it difficult for people to find food.

# FOUR

## REVITALISED

Boats from the oil companies that were building stations throughout the swamp cleared the main flowing watercourses, providing opportunities to catch fish farther away from the local village. As the old man could no longer paddle and catch fish, Sara was now the main provider. Setting off at first sunlight, she would often return with only a few meagre fish that had dried out as she had continued to search for better fishing areas.

She tried to time her return with when the waters from the main river flowed back into the recesses of the swamp, where the higher spits of land were. She would then moor alongside the hut she shared with him, her usual task before attempting to sleep was to place larger logs on the fire in the hope they would still be alight as daylight broke.

The fire was, as usual, very low. Hardly any embers gave off any heat. She slowly built the embers as the flames caught the fine strips of sliced wood. She built the fire with more wood around it until a mass of flames now held off the flies and other insects. She placed a tin filled with swamp water over the fire.

Since he had returned after canoeing through creeks during the worst of the tropical thunderstorms, where he had barely made it back to the lean-to home, he had become even more frail, hardly ever eating his weight seemed to drop from him, nothing she could do seemed to refresh him, so she had yet again taken over the main duties of finding and preparing whatever she could gather from her trips into and through the vast swamp area's.

She looked him over. His breathing was short and raspy, making a gasping sound. He appeared no worse than when she had returned before. He gave a weak wave to acknowledge her.

She had cooled the boiled water, which she gave him with the mashed-up fish and roots she had picked from a jungle tree. Exhausted, he lay back as she slowly washed his face with the remains of the boiled water. He made no movement. He appeared to be at rest.

She slowly climbed back into the canoe before paddling back into the swamp. Again, she thought about what the other women had said, "If your man is not well, give him some of the hyacinth bulb roots, but only when they flower." She had not yet seen any.

# FIVE

# HOPE

As she paddled slowly into the main flow of the swamp, she caught a glimpse of the oil companies' workboats. The white man (recognized throughout swamp area's and locations by the local workers and the company bosses as OGRE meaning boss man), indicated to the local bowswan by moved his hand down, slowing the fast-moving boat. She was only two hundred metres from the spit. She remembered other families lived across the main water flow. This pleased her, as she realised someone was thinking about the jungle-living families.

Her thoughts quickly turned to amazement as the white man's boat turned closer to the opposite side of the main flow. She could just make out a small naked child watching the boat as it passed. Even more astonishment crossed her face as she saw small packages being thrown over the child's head.

The child turned and screeched, joined by others, all of whom ran around picking up the packages. They were all now leaping, jumping, and shouting as they started to open the packages. Their voices were muffled by the sweets they gobbled. She felt saddened because the other jungle families were being given something she had not tasted for many years.

She slowly pulled on the canoe's paddle to continue her search for fish. Again, her head snapped round as the white man's boat turned straight across the main water flow, heading towards the strip of land she had just left. Swiftly she paddled her canoe speedily across the short distance she had just come, arriving just as the white man's boat neared the spit of land. He had watched as she made the return, and he indicated for the local boatman, employed by the companies working in the swamp areas, as a bowswain who always piloted the white man's boat wherever he went at whatever time he required to be moved through any of the swamp areas, to edge closer. He swung two small bags over and into the canoe. They landed in the middle of the canoe. Nothing was lost.

She could see that each bag contained more than one thing. She shouted at the local boatman, who turned and spoke to the white man. His smile said it all. He raised both arms above his head. He shimmied from side to side, clasping both hands as they remained above his head. He shook his hands.

The meaning was obvious. She copied his movement, beaming and laughing as she began to search through the thrown bags.

Later that night, as she spooned a mixture she had made into his mouth, she thought he would get something from the mixture that would help him. His eyes opened as the first spoonful filled his mouth. Again, he opened his mouth. A faint smile touched his face.

Edging backwards, he tried to raise himself. But the effort required was too great. He again sank backward, lying flat on the piece of cloth she had laid him on. But he opened his mouth again.

The mixture she had made was laced with some of the spices that had been in the bags. The mixture only contained a little amount, but it was enough to flavour the usual mixture she fed him.

Slowly, he stopped opening his mouth, lightly shaking his head. She stopped feeding him. His eyes closed as he fell into a deep slumber. She lightly washed his face with a strip of cloth. He never moved.

Before she pulled the paddle out of the mud, she checked him again. His breathing was weak. His scrawny chest just about rose and fell. He moved his head, opening one of his eyes. He watched her as she gathered the lines that held the baited hooks into the canoe; then he watched her as she paddled away.

# SIX

# DEATH

He rolled onto his back. Gasping, he tried to fill his lungs with air. His chest rose as he gulped for more air. No more air entered his body as his chest slowly began to sink back down. Once it reached the same level as the rest of his body, his chest never rose again. All movement left his body as it seemed to flatten out on the piece of cloth. A last gurgling sound came from his half-open mouth. Flies and mosquitoes began to gather over his body, as if they knew he would no longer bother to brush them away.

# Seven
# Removal

Throughout the old man's illness, the village chief had watched her struggle in her efforts to look after and feed the old man. He never once gave her any help, even when he choked and found it extremely difficult to breathe. He just idly watched, knowing the old man would soon pass away. Even as she paddled away as the old man took his last breath, the village chief never moved.

The jungle vegetation swallowed her up as she paddled her canoe into the swamp. The village chief motioned to two of the women who lived with him. Silently, they moved across the short strip of higher ground until they both stood at the lean-to Sara called home. Pulling the old man's body into the open air, they stripped him of his ragged clothes, leaving his naked body spread out. They arranged his arms and legs so they pointed out from his body. The village chief now stood over him, waving the bunch of twigs he carried over each section of the naked body. Turning him over, the women laid the old man's body into a section of muddy earth nearer to the swamp water's edge. The village chief stopped his motions and threw the twigs onto the body, bringing his palm down on his other hand, motioning to the summoned women to commence the ritual that he had been shown by his predecessors before him.

Immediately, the two women brought out the large cutting knives they had hidden in their clothes. Slashing at the joints of his arms and legs, they hacked the old man into pieces. As they separated the sections, they pulled them to the swamp water's edge. They placed the sections slightly apart, arranging them by size, each slightly bigger than the last, until they had completely dismembered the body. Only then, did the older of the women take one of the dismembered joints to the swamp's edge and thrash it around in the water, before placing it again amongst the other dismembered joints.

Clapping his hands, the village chief motioned the women to return with him to the other side of the spit of land. Sitting down, they turned their backs on the grisly sight of the dismembered body.

After all the previous years and the many dead villagers' bodies, it still sickened the village chief to carry out the corpse disposal method he had accepted when he took over running the swamp village. As his previous village chief had said, "Where could we bury any bodies?" There was not and never would be any space to dig a grave—not in the middle of the second-largest jungle in the world. Therefore, they always left it to nature.

Within the jungle's confines, vast numbers of creatures and animals instantly killed and swallowed any unwary jungle dwellers, human or animal. They had therefore left the sections of the old man's body so the jungle creatures would cleanse the waste from the village, as they had repeated over eons. But it did not stop the tears that now ran down the faces of the chief and the two women villagers.

Dimness and darkness came quickly to the jungle swamp, as little light could penetrate the dense vegetation. The village chief had ordered the ever-burning fire to be stacked higher tonight, with a large supply of extra logs, in order to increase the blaze, as the darkness became blackness. Only the shadows of the fire attendants flittered as they placed fresh logs onto the fire.

Suddenly, the jungle noises dropped to total silence. Then and only then could the frightened villagers hear the slap of water. Unseen, the source of the sound seemed to come from many different directions at the same time. Sometimes, the frightened villagers would hear a more solid sound, followed by a large smashing noise that made all of them shiver in fear. More noises could be heard, with throaty grunting cut off by more smashing water sounds. The village chief ordered the women attendants to pile the fire higher, remembering from previous body removals, the fire had burnt down as they rested, the more bold of the jungle creatures had ventured onto the spit of land before they were seen, forever afterwards he remembered this time, thereby knowing that the late-coming animals would be encouraged by the gorging frenzy amongst the jungle animals, who sought out the feeding frenzy on the old man's body, to venture farther onto the higher areas of the jungle's dry land section.

Eventually, faint daylight could be made out through the overhead branches of the jungle trees. For over nine hours, the village fire had been stacked and re-stacked, warding off the feeding frenzy of the jungle animals, mostly crocodiles. Some had moved towards the cluster of the villagers' huts. The villagers drove these crocodiles back into the swamp water by brandishing burning timbers. Smaller rodent creatures scavenged morsels of flesh that had been torn from the larger sections of the body, whilst insects in the billions descended over the blood-strewn earth mound, drawing up any last dregs of bloody moisture, attacking each other in their quest to become the final ones to be sated. Through these actions, the humming, buzzing sound of the insect mass terrified the village chief and the other villagers, for they knew they had no defence against the insects, should they venture away from the water's edge.

As the jungle released its darkness, the village chief slowly moved across the dry spit of high ground, watching for movement from any direction, wary that all the feeding animals had finally left after gorging on the villagers' waste. He could still see small pieces of flesh. Calling over the two women, the chief stayed and watched as they cleared the dry spit of the remnants from the frenzied feeding, sweeping every piece into the swamp waters. Even then, small baby crocodiles rushed in to devour the morsels.

Then, the village chief walked over to the old woman's hut, destroying every bit of the roughly built lean-to, pulling out the four corner posts. The wooden framework collapsed, leaving a pile of ageing wood. He signalled to the women, who moved forward with burning logs, throwing them onto the pile of ageing wood. Quickly, flames burst through the heap. Small animals and insects scurried away from the flames. Finally, the village chief indicated to the two women, who swept the still-burning embers into the swamp waters. Slowly, the embers drifted away, the smoke trails curling down until the swamp water extinguished them.

# EIGHT

# BANISHMENT

Sara had been gone for more than four days, stopping over at other villages out posts, that were dotted throughout the area, some smaller than her home strip of land some much bigger, within the main swamp areas. Every night, she had thought about how he was surviving. She reminded herself of all the other times she had gone away. Somehow, he had gotten through without her. She remembered the time when he had hacked his leg with an axe. He had survived then, so she had continued to paddle the rotten wooden canoe along the edges of the swamp waters, never venturing more than four feet from the banks.

During this trip, sometimes, she saw half-grown crocodiles scurrying away. She traded some fresh crocodile meat she caught for other goods she needed.

Although she was no more than eight miles from her swamp village, she had visited and spent time talking to other families as she made her way through the swamp creeks, always she tried to be away only two some time three days, but this time she had been gone for four days, it took all her effort to paddle against the incoming and outgoing tides that controlled the swamp water levels. Finally, she entered the branch of the swamp that took her towards Makaraba near her village. The tide was lower here, so she put more effort into the paddling.

As she rounded the last bend before the village, her eyes sought out her home. When her eyes caught the emptiness of the space she had lived in, a wailing scream erupted from her, echoing through the jungle branches, piercing through every branch and twig that made up the vegetation of the jungle. It seemed to hang on the very air itself. A second, then a third scream rented the stillness that had descended in the swamp. Nothing moved; even the insects and creatures sensed a tragic scream of despair.

Her eyes continued roving over every section of the swamp area, trying to find what could not be found. She could see the lean-to was not there, but she still did not believe it. She paddled closer to the spit of land, edging the canoe directly toward the point where her home had stood.

The village chief stood up from where he had been watching and waiting for the old woman to return. He motioned for her to move away. He stopped her from reaching the spit of land close to her former home. Shouting at Sara whilst throwing sticks at her, he drove her back into the swamp.

Slowly, she tried again. Again, she was stopped. The water inside the canoe now covered her feet. She reached out her arms, begging the village chief to let her land. Shaking his head, he continued to hold her off. Slowly, she sank back, sticking her paddle into the mud in the swamp water. She quickly tied a piece of cord from the paddle arm to the canoe. Picking up a small rusty tin, she began to bail out the water from her canoe. The village chief spoke quietly to the two women. Both sat down, watching the old woman.

Sara waited for the swamp to become totally black before she slipped out of the canoe and into the swamp water. What meagre food and clothes she had were now the only things in the canoe. As of yet, the water only came just above her knees, but already, tiny and small creatures were attacking her legs, whilst millions of insects kept droning, humming around her head and body. She saw some small crocodiles beginning to edge closer; splashing the water moved them back. She rested her arms in a folded manner, trying to find some rest, but the creatures attacking her below the surface always interrupted these efforts.

Finally, after the total darkness, dim daylight began to filter through. Sara found herself draped over her canoe. Forcing herself upright, she clung onto the canoe's side. Picking through the food bits in the canoe, she swallowed some flakes of fish.

Daylight and movement brought fresh attacks from creatures and insects. With each tide change, she noted that the swamp water rose above her waist, and each tide change brought fresh hazards to her. Clutching the side of her canoe seemed the most sensible option.

Tears began to run down her face as she realised that what had happened so many times before to others was now happening to her. She had seen other villagers' wives forced into the swamp water because their menfolk had passed away or had been knocked out of their canoes only to be taken by any crocodiles that caught them in the swamp water before they could reach the swamp's edges. These other wives had been forced to stand in the water as she now did, this had been the village chief method for as long as she remembered which had also been the practice adopted through out every jungle locations, that did not have access to any main land based burial areas,. No matter how much they had cried or called out, no one had ever gone to the village chief and had them brought back onto the spit of land. Unless they thought that, the women had some use in them—meaning they might be young enough to produce more young children, or just to satisfy their own personal needs—the women were condemned to the fate the jungle had held for over the past eons of years.

No one had ever survived the banishment treatment. At most, they had survived two or three days, before going missing on the fourth. The villagers never heard a noise from the women during these banishments—the condemned women only silently wept.

Sara had rescued a few meagre items from her now-destroyed home. Bitterly, she thought, *Home? What home?* For more years than she could remember, the sticks the old man had pushed into the ground and covered with branches and leaves had been her home.

Dependent on the seasons and the dense, intense jungle surroundings, which since she had been brought to all those years ago never having been taken beyond her earliest village boundaries or to any other sites or locations, she and her man had never gone beyond the only major African town she knew of, Warri which was over fifty miles inside the main swamp areas. There, unless you had money, nothing was available to you—only yourself—making the purchase of useful things impossible. You could usually only buy stale food items, at a price. No one ever got anything unless they paid for it.

Forlornly, she now stood waist-deep off the edge of the dry spit of land where the villagers lived. The village chief sat on his stool placed in the centre of the dry spit. He sat facing where the old woman stood in the swamp. Never moving or speaking, he would order drinks and food from the other villagers by gesturing with his hand. Constantly, she pleaded with the village chief. He never offered her help or food; he just sat waiting and watching.

Since she had returned, the village area had been banned to her. Some of the other village women circled around the edge of the dry spit of land, hoping to throw morsels of food to her. Each time the scraps of food landed in the swamp water, they were eagerly swallowed by the small animals and fought over by the insects. Each time, the village chief just smiled. Slowly, he drew a line in the mud, recording the days the old woman had lasted.

With the passing of daylight to darkness, she had now seen two days pass. The usual daily life of the swamp and jungle had gone on. Early every day, the stream of launches and boats had continued to pass the jungle villages on both sides of the main stream of muddy water as each tide forced water into the swamp areas, before ebbing out of the same water flows. She had seen the boats going to the oil platform being built only nine hundred metres away, and had also seen them leaving every night before it got dark. Still, the village chief sat staring at the old woman, and nothing changed, except the water began to feel much colder at night.

The small swamp creatures were now becoming bolder, scrabbling around her feet under the water. Tears streamed down her face. Also, her hands had begun to lose feeling, so she tied her hand to the canoe in case she fell over. She remembered a day when, as a little girl, she played with the other children in her home village. She had been happy then—with a home, a family, no cares or worries—until the day she had been taken at only nine years old. Remembering this time made her feel totally sad, for she now knew her time would soon end.

Lightness began to etch its way through the overhead canopy of the jungle trees. Already warm at this early hour, again, Sara heard the boats coming. No longer able to stand without leaning over her canoe, she struggled to twist her head round so she could see which boat was passing. Pain racked her body; the weakness caused by standing in the swamp water made her eyes become weaker. She started to gently moan; she called her mother although she hardly knew who she was. Too many days and years had passed to remember.

Sara could easily feel the swamp creatures nibbling at her feet and legs. She could no longer make them move away. She had also seen the larger croc is moving ever closer. Only by moving the canoe paddle she had tied to the mooring pole she and her man had used for many years, she had to replace the paddle with the pole as she had dropped the paddle when she had slid off the canoe edge, using the pole she could stop them from edging even closer. Her eyes were constantly shedding tears, but none ever ran down her face. The village chief remained sitting at the edge of the swamp, knowing it would not be long now before she fell off the canoe and disappeared beneath the swamp water.

# NINE

# REVIGORATION

The oil companies' workboat had slowed down, edging closer to the spit of land where the kids lived. As usual, it pushed nearer to the tiny spit of high ground opposite the chief's village. Small parcels of food and sweets were thrown to the children. They scrambled for the gifts, immediately filling their mouths, laughing and shouting as the boat pulled away. Waving and whooping, they watched as the boat moved towards the spit of high ground where the village chief sat.

The local boatman shouted to the village chief. On the second call, the village chief got up and walked towards the boat. A deep conversation took place. The village chief kept waving his arm back towards the old woman. Each time, he, the launches pilot, asked the village chief to intercede on behalf of the old woman, it was answered with a firm shake of his head. The white man had listened to all this discussion, brought up his hand, and rubbed his finger and thumb together. Immediately, the village chief held up his hand with three fingers showing. The boatman looked at the white man, who held up one and a half fingers, tilting his head from side to side. At last, the village chief smiled, nodding, and money changed hands.

Another discussion briefly took place. One more finger was held up by the village chief who also using; his hand made a circle twice. The white man nodded. All raised their hands and clasped them together. They had agreed on everything.

The village chief moved over to where the old woman still clung onto the canoe. Waving his arm, he motioned for her to come closer. Rapidly, he explained to her that she could now move her canoe back to the spit of high ground. Already he had called to the other village men to fetch poles and banana leaves, which they were now shaping and pushing into the semi-muddy surface. She still stood alongside her canoe as though it were an item of her independence. The small piece of cord still attached her to the canoe. The canoe always reminded her of the man she had lived with.

She had nodded off into a light sleep when the village chief grasped her shoulder. Panicking, she began to struggle away from him until he pointed to a newly built lean-to shack. Untying the cord from her wrist, he led her to the building. Speaking rapidly in the local dialect, he explained this was now her home for as long as she lived. Bewildered, she stared at him. Pointing to her chest, she asked, "Mine?" His nodding head and broad smile gave her the answer.

Turning, he then pointed to her canoe. Two village men were now pulling it away. Screaming, she tried to move after it. Again, the village chief grasped her arm and, sitting her down, explained what she had not heard. Gradually, her tears were replaced with a look of amazement as he told her the white man had been extremely upset, seeing her always stood in the swamp water, so he had ordered the village chief to rebuild her home and to make her a new canoe, which the village men who fashioned canoes were now building.

After three more days, in which the village chief had provided her with water and food, there was a new canoe gently floating close to the rebuilt forest home. Eagerly, Sara tried sitting in the high seat of the canoe. She noted that the canoe builders had also layered the bottom of the canoe with sweated-on leaves, making the canoe even more watertight.

Her face was now always fixed with a happy, broken-tooth grin. Never had she imagined that she would be happier than when she first moved to this location as a bought young girl who would function for the man buyer a she began to grow older, all those years ago. Each morning, she would wake up and see her canoe gently bobbing in the slightly moving jungle waters. She could now choose when to fish, or maybe she would visit other swamp villages that dotted every creek. No more would she have to rely on other villagers to remain on the lookout for her, in case her old canoe became flooded. Never had she felt happier.

Often, she would hear the boats from the oil companies passing both up and down from the platforms. She seemed to always miss seeing the white man's boat go past, although she knew it had come there, as he left small parcels of food outside her home. No longer did the other villagers steal the food parcels; the village chief had given instructions. Some days there were parcels, some days there were none, but always the next day, there would be more parcels, she also noted that the village chief was more giving to the other villagers, as other parcels of foods were also left for him, he did not ever mention of the old woman's ordeal, but he never again spoke harshly to her.

Now more content, she often paddled her canoe down the smaller creeks to catch fish, first making sure that she saw no crocodiles in sight. Fishing in these small creeks was safer than fishing in the large, open creeks. It was only then she sometimes caught sight of the white man's boat. Each time she did, she would stand up in the middle of her canoe with her paddle in both hands. She would let out a piercing scream, jigging her hips from side to side, in an opposite movement to her arms. Every time the white man heard the scream, he would immediately copy her movement as he placed his hands over his head, waving to her with clasped-hand gestures. She always replied by copying his clasped hands. Slowly, as time went on, everywhere the white man's boat went, everyone copied these gestures, it became the national way of greeting whilst fishing for food.

As she travelled through the swamp's creeks, she heard that the white man's boat was always moving everywhere through the swamps—some days at the nearest platform, sometimes at a very distant platform, but the small parcels of food always kept coming. Because of these extra food rations, she was able to conserve some of the fish she caught. She would hoard it in safe places, making sure it would not get wet during monsoon season. She had never liked this time of year, as sometimes, the rains were unrelenting.

As the rainy season took hold, it restricted her fishing trips, making her rely on any food she had stored up. Slowly, as the weather closed in, she was forced to sit out each rainy period in her home, only just managing to stay out of the main rains. Her mind would go to what the white man was doing, for now more than ever, she could constantly hear the boats go past.

# TEN

# CHANGES

Each and every morning, due to changes the oil companies had made, the boats and launches were now required to travel from the main swamp town of Warri. This added over an hour to daily travel, whilst reducing the number of boats servicing the swamp platforms, which meant that instead of travelling directly to each swamp platform, they had to start at the river entrance to the swamp, servicing each platform as they came to it. This extended travel time throughout the swamp and also made it more hazardous now that the rainy seasons had begun. Each morning, the changeover crews huddled under the boats' canopies, trying to avoid the constant rainstorms, usually with little success. The white man's boat always seemed to carry more crewmembers than other boats, because he seldom ever stopped off, calling at the swamp's side villages.

Since his intervention with the village chief, the white man had daily-sought signs of the old woman during his travels, sometimes catching a glimpse of her as she paddled her new canoe through the swamp's branch streams. This would result in her waving and jigging in her canoe. He always waved back to her. Now, throughout the tropical rainstorms, he had never really seen her, only a hard-to-see hunched-over figure because of the torrential downpour. Also, as he tried to keep dry whilst travelling through the swamp during these downpours, sometimes a strong wind blew through the swamp, causing waves to flow through the swamp tributaries creeks that meandered everywhere throughout the swamp areas. When this happened, you would have to stop in the calmest place you could find, sometimes having to enter the quietest creeks. This was where the crocodiles would usually rest.

# ELEVEN

## Tropical Storm

Sara was out in the main swamp stream when a storm hit the swamp. Quickly, she paddled to the nearest opening in the swamp vegetation, finding a small creek. Once through the screening branches, she pushed her paddle into the soft mud. Covering herself with a plastic sheet, she sat down to wait for the storm to pass. The fish she had netted as she rushed to the creek began to thrash about alongside her canoe. Braving the rainstorm, she began to pull the netted fish into the canoe. It was a large fish. She struggled to get it over the edge of the canoe. Straining with her feet against the canoe's side, she gradually eased the fish into the lowest part of her canoe. It fell more quickly as she still strained on the net. Then, it totally flopped inside the canoe.

# TWELVE

## DESPERATE TIMES

As a crocodile made a grab for the fish, it flipped Sara's canoe over, throwing her over eight feet away from the canoe. Feeling the heavy reverberation of breaking water, the crocodile spun round towards the sound. Sara's arm broke the surface as she gasped for air. Instantly, the crocodile was at her. She managed to hit the snout, which stopped the creature from grasping her. She reached for the canoe, which had glided nearer to her. Managing to grasp the canoe's side and heave herself up, she hung over the canoe's edge.

The croc had stopped short of her, watching as she struggled to reach the canoe. Now, as she lay half-in and half-out, it again attacked her, clamping down on her legs, which still trailed in the swamp water. Rolling over, the crocodile pulled one of her legs out of its joint, tearing the flesh as it did so, backing off as it tried to swallow the severed limb. Pulling herself up even harder, Sara managed to flop into the canoe's bottom. Peering over the canoe's side, she watched as the crocodile finally swallowed her leg. Grabbing her paddle, she began to push the canoe out of the creek. The effort and blood loss made her feel very light-headed, causing her to black out as she made the main creek's water flow.

# THIRTEEN

# BY THE SHORT FOUR MILES

As she was struggling to overcome her difficulties, the white man had just arrived at the entrance to the swamp off the Warri River. The tropical storm had made it extremely difficult to navigate the entrance. The cloud base was only six feet above the river level. Streaming rain and the crash of thunder-lessened visibility. Finding the entrance to the creek took the effort of his launch's entire crew.

# FOURTEEN

## DESPERATE RESCUE

The crew could now see the reed bed's split. As the launch eased its way forward, the Nigerian boatman increased the launch's speed. Faintly, between the crashes of thunder, a piercing scream caused the crew to look around. Against the backdrop of the reed screen, two local canoes were silhouetted in the flashing lightning could be made out. The local tribeswomen were splashed water that was pouring in, out of the canoes, trying to keep them afloat, but rapidly, they were losing the battle. The white man pointed to the canoes. The Nigerian boatman eased the launch towards the two canoes.

Each canoe was piled high with logs that the women had collected; before the storm had reached them each had a child sat on top of the wood. As the launch neared the first canoe, the screaming woman picked up her child. Her efforts rocked the canoe, which immediately turned over, dumping all the wood into the swamp. Both the young child and the woman disappeared under the water.

Observing what was happening, the white man immediately dived over the launch's side, pushing aside the half-sunken logs. He made out the young child's small arm. Grabbing the child's arm, he pushed back to the surface, hoisting the child over the side of the launch. Where the mesmerized crew had waited, breathing deeply he dived again towards the reed bed's edge, where normally the young and older crocodiles congregated, pushing aside his thoughts he vaguely made out the struggling form of the local woman. Grasping her arm, he pulled her to the surface. The launch was now twenty-five metres away, but was coming towards him as the local boatman searched the swamp surface for him.

As the launch reached him he placing his arm on the launch's edge, the white man heaved the rescued local woman onto board. The Nigerian boatman was pointing the launch away from him, so as the white man held on to the edge of the launch, it dragged him towards the other heavily loaded local canoe. As he shouted at the other local woman to throw all the wood out of her canoe, the launch began to close in on the canoe. Again, this woman tried to throw her child onto the launch. The launch, which was still moving, pushed the child away. The white man saw this; he plucked the child out of the swamp water and threw him over his arm and into the launch. As this canoe began to sink, the woman pushed away from the sinking canoe. Now naked to the waist through her efforts offloading the sticks, she thrashed towards the white man, who grasped her wrist as she came nearer, dragging her towards the launch, which had been edging closer. Grasping the launch's edge with one hand, he hoisted her into the launch, where she flopped onto the launch's decking.

The white man's efforts had retrieved the local women from the swamp. Whilst he had pushed the second woman into the launch, he noted and saw a small rope around her wrist. He pulled the rope from her arm. As a result, the local woman's canoe bobbed to the surface, empty of the logs. Passing the rope up to the launch's driver, he was pulled aboard, and made sure the rope and canoe were tied tight. Then, the launch made its way back to the villagers' home on the only dry spit of land around.

The launch's arrival at the villagers' camp caused a considerable uproar. As the rescued villagers ran into the tribal section of their village, many voices could be heard shouting, followed by cheering. Whole sections of the village people rushed towards the launch, bringing with them much food and large jugs of drink. The white man ordered the launch to back off as soon as the villagers were safely on the dry spit of land, so as the people rushed to the launch, more than forty metres away, the crew and workers all waved. As the launch turned and sped away, the villagers' lamenting shouts grew louder. The whole village population stood begging for the launch to return. Signalling to the boatman, the white man ordered the launch to continue towards Odidi, the first platform manned by the launch operators. As the launch disappeared through the reed curtain, the shouting of the villagers still followed the launch.

# FIFTEEN

# DETERMINATION

Meanwhile, as she struggled to guide her canoe, the old woman, between periods of blackout, managed to get the canoe into the Makaraba creek. The incoming tide helped push it towards her local village. Slowly, with some thrusts of her paddle, the canoe made it to the section of the turnoff to her village.

It was the village chief who first saw her, slumped over the edge of her canoe. Rising quickly, he began to move towards the slowly moving canoe. Suddenly, he stopped. As the canoe reached the dry spit, the water movement continued, and the crocodile switched its tail. Swiftly stepping back, the crocodile lunged at the stopped canoe. As he saw the crocodile's full size, the village chief slumped back. Looking longer than five metres, the croc again lunged at the canoe. Its large, open jaws clamped down on the canoe's side with a tremendous crash, splitting the canoe in two, which impaled Sara's body with a shaft of timber.

As the croc began to roll over, dragging the ruined canoe into the main stream, Sara's body again surfaced. A hand seemed to wave as the croc again rolled over. Then, the water became still; no movement could be seen. The villagers who had caught the final act of the crocodile attack all huddled together behind the village chief. He still stood as he had stopped, but now, tears streamed down his face.

Suddenly, a huge splash came from the water. One end of the canoe resurfaced, showing the terrible marks of the crocodile attack. Gentle now, it bobbed in the jungle stream before it suddenly sank.

Two days later, the white man's launch was on its way to Makaraba when it stopped off at the village's dry spit of land. The village chief stood at the water's edge as the launch came to a halt. Listening to the village chief and the local boatman, the white man became aware that something was not right. The old woman's home was no longer standing; her canoe was not tied to the pole. She was not there. The village chief held out his hand; many paper money notes could be seen.

The local launch boatman finished his discussion with the village chief. He explained to the white man all that the village chief had told him. The white man listened intently, with his head bowed. Even after the story had been related to him, the white man kept his head bowed. Finally, he lifted his head and smiled at the village chief. Clasping his hands in front of his face, he bowed his head to the village chief. He then ordered the village chief to keep the money, with the promise that the village chief hold a village party for the old woman. This was agreed.

After he had completed his work at Makaraba, the white man began his trip back to Jones Creek, which was the main natural gas compressor station throughout the swamp work had been ongoing for several years starting off as a joke, the white man had nominated the Jones Creek bush bar as the three star pub of the swamp areas (constructed out of tree trunks and platted reeds as a Three Star Bush Bar, the local beer brewed was made by the Star Beer Company, who used that particular symbol for their bottle tops), stopping only at the dry spit of land. He called the village chief over, and through the local boatman, he explained what he wanted. The village chief took the items the boatman gave to him.

Consequently, should any people question or disbelieve that these events ever happened, then it is politely suggested that they visit that site, or the bush bar at Jones Creek, where they can still see these nailed-on trophies. These trophies are bottle tops, indicated by stars. Jones Creek has three stars, and the jungle location has five stars.

www.ingramcontent.com/pod-product-compliance
Lightning Source LLC
Chambersburg PA
CBHW051420250726
48655CB00003B/1147